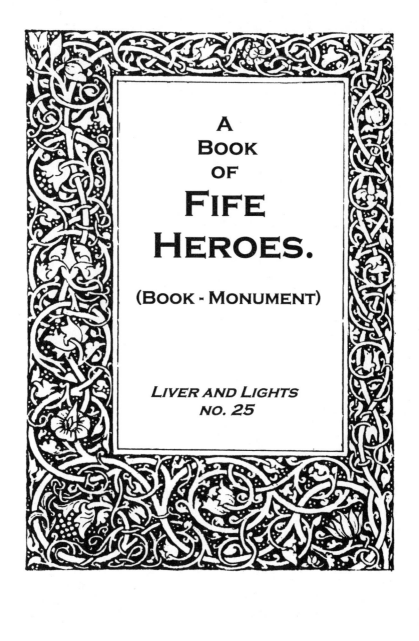

A
BOOK
OF
FIFE
HEROES.

(BOOK - MONUMENT)

*LIVER AND LIGHTS
NO. 25*

A Book of Fife Heroes
(Book Monument).

Compiled, designed and devised by **John Bently**

Copyright. The contributors and John Bently

ISBN 0-9533961-0-X

**British Library Cataloguing in Publication Data.
A catalogue record for this book is available
from the British Library.**

Printed in Great Britain by Redwood Books,
Kennet House, Kennet Way, Trowbridge, Wiltshire
BA 14 8RN
(0125 769979)

Published by
**Liver and Lights Scriptorium
101 Upland Rd
London
SE22 0DB**

Liver and Lights No. 25.
December 1st 1998

THE SCOTTISH **ARTS** COUNCIL

National Lottery Fund

Fife

C O U N C I L

For all the children,
but particularly Arthur.................

**pecial thanks** are due to all the people I was privileged to meet during the course of this books compilation and in particular the students and staff of Collydean School, Glenrothes, Kirkcaldy North Primary School, Sinclairtown Primary School, East Wemyss Primary School and Falkland Primary School. In addition, all those helpers and energetic children in various after - school establishments: the MAD Kids club,Buckhaven, the Rio Centre, Kirkcaldy and the Dolphin Centre, Tayport.

Particular individual thanks are also due to David Swift, artist -in - residence at Lynnebank Hospital, Caroline Clark at the Rio Centre, Gillian Waring, Mrs McQuillan and Mrs Abernethy at Kirkcaldy North. Leslie Burrell, Head of Collydean School, and all the other fine teachers and pupils who spared me some of their precious time but whose names I have unforgivably mislaid. Thanks and apologies are also due to all the people who, for one reason or another, find their contributions have been cut from the final book. Particular thanks in this respect to Mrs Mary Birrell, MBE, at the Wemyss School of Needlework and Henry Shanks, of Eastercash Farm, Falkland who were thwarted by the inadequacies of my primitive tape recorder.

A Special Big thank you to Babs McCool for instigating the project and Lesley O'Hare for carrying on the work. Also to Dawn Murray, Bobby and Ron for being so patient with my impossible demands.

Finally, a big medal to Emily Wood for services to typing, Damien Gascoine for use of his overheated photocopier and a newly minted Good Wife trophy to Charlotte, who somehow had to cope with my many absences from home, in search of the ultimate shopping list.....

A

B

he original idea behind this project was to design a piece of 'Public Art' using The Kingdom of Fife as raw reference material whilst involving as many people as possible in the actual processes of it's manufacture. This piece of art would not be yet another mural, nor another town square sculpture, but something everyone could own a piece of. Something which would cost a fiver, but whose true value would be infinite and inconceivable. In short, a book.

For twenty years or so my working life has been wholly inspired by the idea of The Book as a vehicle for creative experimentation. Central to this activity has been the belief that books are vessels which store and administer ideas through time into posterity and that even the most mundane of them hold crucial messages for the future.

With this in mind, I devised a scheme whereby I would ask as many people as humanly possible in Fife a few simple questions:

Is there a hero in your family? Can you tell me what makes them special? Can you illustrate your story in some way? The answers to these questions would provide the core material from which the book would be built.

C

Adverts in the local press initially produced a less than lively response from Fife's adult population. Then, I went into schools and asked children the same questions. Here, undoubtedly, I came across the heart of Fife. Their enthusiasm and hope for the future has formed the finished work you now hold. All the children and teachers I met were a great credit to the education system in this country and deserve praise to be heaped upon them.

Also, I asked each person I met to draw a portrait of someone else in the room. This produced a bank of over 1000 drawings of contemporary Fife residents. Most of those I have used here have been deliberately detached from their names. I must admit to deliberate mischief in this respect: I thought it would be fun for you to try and see how many faces you recognised. My apologies to the artists I have rendered anonymous (There is a complete list elsewhere in the book.)

Incidentally, most people initially swore blind they 'couldnae draw'. We must allow the aforementioned posterity to be the judge of that.

My own personal belief, central to the creation of this book, and strengthened through years of experience teaching drawing to people of widely varying ages and supposed abilities, not to mention 30-odd years as a practitioner, is that a 'drawing' is no more, no less than an idea expressed visually. A drawing's success in achieving this is the only true criterion for judging it's success or failure. There are no rules for 'good' or 'bad' drawing. Like everything in life (and Art), we make up the rules as we go along, or run the risk of having them made up for us. Artists are merely people who realise this. Everyone can be an artist.

The other illustrations are things collected from the streets of places I visited. Bus tickets, photos, graffiti, torn up letters, and the things that for me tell the real story of contemporary Fife…..shopping lists. You are what you buy! The lists we make cannot lie! I apologise to anybody who recognises their handwriting.

Later, after the book had been printed, we would invite all the contributors back to add something by hand to every single copy. They would stick- in photo's, hand- colour illustrations, rubber stamp text and so forth - a genuine cottage industry.

Finally, I would like to say that I think, in some way, everyone is a hero. Everyone alive is a survivor in a great adventure. I've said more than enough. In the remainder of this book, the people of Fife will do all the talking……………

John Bently.   August 1st 1998

E

John Adie (Sinclairtown)

My great grandad was called John Adie. He was in the second World War. He shot a lot of guys. He drove an army truck, I think. He didn't die, he came home.

When he was digging a pit for my gran and grandad he had a heart attack. My gran lifted him up and took him into the living room, but he died. This all happened before I was born, I never got to meet him.

Micheal Moore (Collydean)

My dad was a Kart driver at Knockhill when he was twenty years old. He retired when he was 24. He is now 41 and working in the Rosyth dockyard and he is a sparky. He has overcome a lot of obstacles.

Rachel Kirkbride. (Sinclairtown)

My Auntie Ella was a Nurse. She played Crazy Golf and competed in competitions. When she broke her leg she made up a poem. It goes like this:

Ella Peggy lost her leggy
in amongst the snow
and when she went
to look for it
she lost herself an' o.

Now she is 70 and we go to her house every school morning. We usually go over to stay nights and we have lots of fun. She is my Special Auntie and I love her very much. She has a very long name and is excellent at knitting. When she was at school the Germans were here so she couldn't go out to play. Her name is Isabela Simsin Bogi Madravi Peggy.

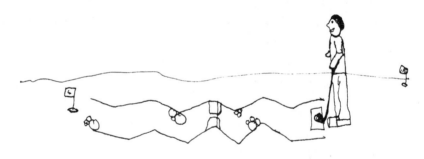

4

My DaD in the army

My DaD Joined the army wen he was 16. he had a accident on the head. So he disent rmembat a lot a bowt it. he had some frends wen he was ther he had a uniform it was a hat a Jacket and trwsers. he wars glasses. he drivd a van for the army. he lefffd wen he was 27. he some times forget arthur things. his unisarm was green. he was in the scootish army. and now he is 47. he went around the world. he has brvown hat. THE END

So now he works a fife council asa Road worker. diging roads up. and taking slabs up now.

Dad

by Stephanie Stewart

5

Craig Young (Collydean)

My special hero is my Dad because he went to Africa to help the sick children and adults. He was going to another place when the he got past the guards at the gate about five soldiers ran around the front of the truck and shot the driver. Then two opened the door to see if anyone was in the back and my father was in the back with his friend sorting out the supplies of food. When they heard the bang they got a shock and my dad's friend got shot in the foot and my dad was panicking but the driver was still alive. The driver drove away from the ambush and then he died, but he saved my dad and his friend.

Another special hero is my mum because she was in a car crash. I was coming back from the doctors because I had to get a permission slip for tablets. We were on the way to school and she said "Let's turn round the roundabout", because we live just down from the school. When we got to the opening of Rockfield Gdns this woman just came from nowhere and crashed into us. I was so much in shock I stayed in the seat for half an hour in the same spot. I never moved one muscle. My mum has been in pain for over eight months since the car crashed into us.

7

Leslie Fraser (Kirkcaldy North)

My friend Ryan has saved the lives of two people. He is only eleven.

One of the lives he saved was mine.

We were playing at the railway so Ryan decided to cross it so I agreed. Both of us crossed one track. Just as I was about to cross the next one, Ryan noticed a train very close to us and going very quickly. Ryan quickly grabbed me and hauled me off the line. My heart was beating so fast I could hear it in my head. I've never been to the railway since...

The other life he saved was Sean Binnie's life. Ryan came over to Sean's house at night to see Sean. Sean was trying to fix his dads cable box.Suddenly Sean was pulling the two wires together and he got electrocuted. Ryan thought he was only kidding until he smelt burning. Ryan quickly took the plug out and Sean's mum rushed him to hospital. 240 volts were going through him. The last words Sean said before he went to hospital was "Ryan, you're my hero".

```
*****        KWIK SAVE        *****
VAT NO 107 4212 12 -STORE1162


       CARRIER BAGS              .01
*****             SUB-TOTAL      .01

       CASH                      .01
       CHANGE                    .00

TOTAL ITEMS 1
22/08/98 17:18 1162507 0168 13979
KWIK SAVE NO NONSENSE FOODSTORES
*** THANK YOU FOR YOUR CUSTOM **
```

12

Craig Early (Sinclairtown)

My Dad is called Greg Early. This is a story about him going from the bottom to the top (almost) of football. It all started when he was young. He loved football so he made a career out of it. He played for the juniors and he went to five-a-side games and played for East Fife. He quitted because he broke his collar-bone, knee, knuckle, leg, arm (both), nose and nails (all). He ended up a quarry manager. Here's a wee poem about him:

My Dad was right at the top
of the football business.
He was number nine in the
dressing room, his team mates say
ohh what a glorious goal!
Top left corner
ripped the net!
How can ye no' break a leg
whammin' ba's like that!
What a tackle that boy did,
you got a free kick. You absolutely
whammed it.
The crowd at their brim
were just hoping it would go in.
When the goalie saved it,
the crowd just went blank.
Then the ninety minute whistle blew
with the score at 2-1,
The crowd went ooh - noo'
and that was the end.

James Mc Bain (Collydean)

My special Hero is my Mum for being strong with her disease and she didn't let that get her down. She also didn't let anyone help her in any way through the treatment. I think she showed me that life goes on, even if you faced illness or death. My Mum (Lorna) lived in Woodside.

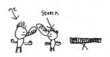

Michael S. (Sinclairtown)

My best friend's name is Steven Kirk. He is my best friend and always will be. We play together at break and lunch. We make songs at break and lunch. We don't play football, we just make songs. And we are going to be famous. One day.

Charlie Duncan (Sinclairtown)

My mum's friends boy is a Raith Rovers player. He is a very good player. He is the youngest in the team. I do not know him. My mum is the only one who knows him in my family. My mum tells me if he scores. My mum tells me when he scores. He had scored 31 times in his life. 18 breakaways and 13 ordinaries. He is my hero.

April

Debit   Credit

Allan Maguire (East Wemyss)

The most favourite friend I have is God. I like him that much because he's always good to me and he always guides me when I'm getting bullied or anything bad. I know he's guiding me because the pain doesn't last long.   I will always remember him when I am getting bullied it really hurts my feelings. I don't know what he looks like but I know what angels look like, well I think I know... they have wings and they're white.

Fife found portraits: **Kirkcaldy**

Craig J Seath.

My Grandfather, John Farries.

"Plunged into an icy river to rescue child" ran the front page headline.

In 1931 John Farries was a 39 year old baker with the Co-operative society in Lochgelly.
Jack, as he preferred to be called, had served in the Seaforth Highlanders in India and saw action in WW1 in France, before settling down to his chosen trade of Baker back in Scotland.
Early in 1931 he was taking a two day holiday visiting his father in Montrose, and it was during this break that he was fated to meet young Sheila Knox.

A new bridge had been built over the estuary and Jack had expressed an interest in taking a walk to view the construction. Accompanied by his father-in law and brother-in-law, he took a leisurely stroll, not aware of the drama ahead. As they reached the bridge their attention was drawn to what they at first thought was a dog in the water. As they watched, interest turned to horror as they realised it was in fact a small girl, tossed around in the debris of the demolished temporary bridge.. Mindless of his own danger from the debris and biting cold, Jack plunged in, grabbed hold of her, swung her over his shoulder and made his way back to the bank. Jack's bother-in-law had found an old piece of rope and vainly tried to get them out. Somehow, Jack made it to the bank and handed the trembling girl over to her cousin.
Jack was presented with an inscribed gold watch by the Cowdenbeath bakers union in recognition of his bravery..

Sheila was only three years old at the time of her rescue, but never forgot Jack, visiting him on many occasions at his home in Kelty before his death in 1984.

```
            SOMERFIELD LEVEN
   TEL NO.01333 424209 VAT NO.107 4212
   YOUR STORE MANAGER IS ALAN BRUCE
   YOU WERE SERVED TODAY BY PAMELA

      WE WOULD VALUE YOUR COMMENTS
      ABOUT YOUR SHOPPING TRIP
          TO THIS STORE TODAY,
          PLEASE LET US KNOW.

          SOMERFIELD
      SHOPPING IN THE
          REAL WORLD


                                     £
          SF CRISPS            1.39
          V-TUALLY F-F         0.89
          THICK BREAD          0.39
          SF MINCE             0.99
     ****            TOTAL      3.66
          CASH                20.00
          CHANGE              16.34

   TOTAL NUMBER OF ITEMS SOLD =  4
   15/06/98 15:38 2116 05 0244 161
          SOMERFIELD STORES LIMITED
      WHITCHURCH BRISTOL BS14 0TJ
```

Jennifer (Falkland)

I Wish xhe qeen livd in fife.

Andrew Clark. (Falkland)

Once, about two or three years ago me and my brother were playing happily on the swings in my garden. But we were going so high with no nails on the swings that it tipped over! I was very frightened because I fell hard and the bars fell on me. I could hardly breathe! My brother just got out of the way in time. I was shouting for help and as he heard me he was strong enough to lift the bars up and set me free. Me and my brother are not exactly best friends but now we know not to go to high on the swings!

The final race

Nadine Miyasar. (Sinclairtown)

My dad, mum and me lived in Iraq when I was little. My dad was a runner in races. My mum was an ordinary house wife and I was the centre of attention. This is all about my dad and his career. It all started when he was in high school. There was a running course that he usually went to at break time. At high school he ran in the start races and won some of them. Then after school one day at my dad's home he got a phone call saying that he was chosen to represent his school in the race for the best runner. So off he went to the race. The first race was close. He nearly fell.

The second one was also close. Every time it was closer. At the end of the final race my dad won with another boy, so they had to do a race together. Off they went like speeding light. First my dad then the other boy. It was so close. Finally my dad won. He got the gold medal. So that was the start of his career.

25

Evette Allan. (Sinclairtown)

My gran use to work in the navy. She started when she was 20. She is my favourite person in my family. She worked on the planes with a friend. She put the parachutes in the planes. And fixed the engines if they ever got broken. One day she was eating her dinner when she saw a man so she went up to him and said "Do you like my hair?". He said "Yes its lovely." So the next day he went over to her to get some salt. She noticed him. So the next day they got together and had dinner together and he said why don't we get together again. She said yes. So the next time they got together. He said why don't we get married. She said yes. So a few months later they got married and they had my mum. My grandad has died but my gran is still here.

Craig Henderson. (Collydean)

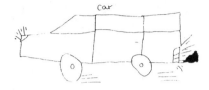

My Auntie was in a very bad car crash one very foggy night and she went straight into a big ditch. The firemen could not find her because she was in the ditch but when they found her they had to cut her free from the car and that took about an hour to do and then she got taken to the hospital and then she was in the hospital for a couple of days and when she got out she was on crutches for a couple of weeks and then she took the crutches back and then she was OK.

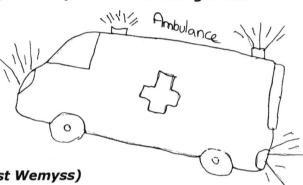

Scott Wilson. (East Wemyss)

I like my grandad because he made a train set for me when I was a baby and he brought me in to liking trains. He and I made a train set together. I have now got it in my room, he is roundabout sixty, and he has retired. He used to live down in Cheltenham in England.

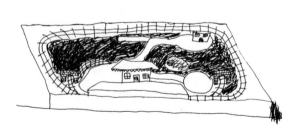

Alistair Harra (Kirkcaldy North)

My grandad is called Jimmy and he used to be in the army. His job was a mine sweeper. He used to tell me stories about when he was in the war. He said there was always sirens going off and air wardens coming round houses telling people to get into their air shelters in the back garden. He said the air shelters were little rooms about three to four foot under the ground with a metal roof over it. He told me about when he felt the ground with a knife for mines. He gave my gran his medals. He has some gold ones which my gran tells me are for his bravery. I could imagine him in a green uniform with black shoes and a helmet. He never killed any one in the war. There was always a bit of magic when he told me his stories. I always looked forward to the day when my grandad came. He died four years ago. I was very sad when he died.

Christopher McKellar (Collydean)

My favourite person is my Mum because she saved a man's life. She did so by calming him down. He came in shouting and roaring about how he was going to set himself alight. In the end, my Mum calmed him down and wiped him clean.

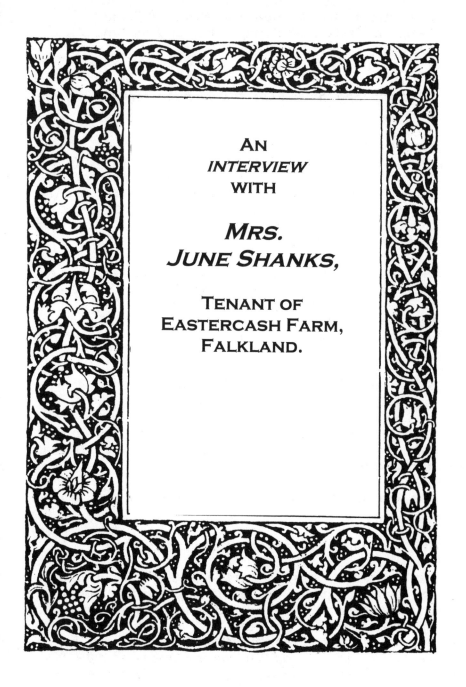

AN
INTERVIEW
WITH

MRS.
JUNE SHANKS,

TENANT OF
EASTERCASH FARM,
FALKLAND.

Transcript of an interview with Mrs June Shanks.
Tenant of Eastercash Farm, Falkland, Fife. June 5th
1997

JB. *How long have your family been farming in this area ?*

Mrs Shanks: *Well.. since 1907. My Father-in-law, he was in the Boer war... went when he was 17. He was going to join the British Army, but he was too young, so he joined the Cape Mounted Rifles and fought there and his father died (he owned a construction firm) so Grandfather Shanks had to come back and tidy things up and he decided to take a year on a farm in Buckhaven.*

So, eventually, he came here, to Eastercash, and met his future wife ...who fell in love with him because of his leather breeches! He had already taken Falkland Wood (in 1907), so he came, with his mother, and got married in 1910 and they had five sons and one daughter and I married one of the sons! Ha ha ha!

So... that was how long we've been on the estate.
We don't own the farm - we're tenants.

JB: *I noticed that there was a big sign further up that said 'Farm Shop - organic vegetables for sale' Is that part of this farm ?*

Mrs Shanks: *No - that's part of the Estate - it does terribly well....*

JB: *Are they a Big Family that owns the Estate ?*

Mrs Shanks : *It's the Crichton-Stuart's. The original owner, the Marquis of Bute, came here in 1887 and took the estate and all its tenants. When he died he left it to, not his eldest son, because he inherited the title and the family pile at Bute, but his second son, Lord Ninian Crichton Stuart, but he went off to fight in World War One, and was killed in 1915, so it was kept kicking over with Factors and people until his son was old enough.*

(He never saw the son that took over from him-he died in October 1915 and his son was born in March when he was away - very sad...)

And then....now, it's under Trustees.

Lord Ninian's son, Michael - which happens a lot- had difficulty running the estate. The National Trust took it over in the 1950's

JB: *Any connection with the Royal Stuarts? Are they Pretenders, these Stuarts ?*

Mrs Shanks: *Ha, Ha, Ha ! Well..........No... I've never heard them say that!*
My son Henry, of course, is the third generation of Shanks at Eastercash, which is a bit unusual for a family who came here in 1907. But I'm from Falkland, just down the road... I'm completely Fife . My family came from Kirkcaldy.

JB: *What was your maiden name ?*

Mrs Shanks: *It's Brodie.   My Father - He was an engineer- left school at 12..   He was completely self educated; went into a draughtsman's office at 12-13; went into a business and after working his way through eventually took the business over. I don't know if that happens nowadays - well you're not allowed to leave school at 12, anyway!*

So- he worked his way up from nothing as an apprentice and eventually owned the factory.
His father was just a warehouseman.
Anyway-what they did was make the machines which printed the linoleum.

Kirkcaldy linoleum

They were called Melville, Brodie. You learn that at school. Melville was his partner. He died and Dad got his share.

JB: *So much of the industry around Kirkcaldy seems to be based on Linoleum...*

Mrs Shanks: *Oh Yes... a tremendous industry at one time. I think there's only one factory left now... Nairns... they've recently started making Linoleum again...they made all the lino for ships - different types, thick stuff for factories and thin for houses. I think people are beginning to realise what fantastic stuff it is. Incredibly hard wearing. We've got some in the house that has been here since 1923 !*

JB: *So...you're Grandfather was a warehouseman-do you know anything about your Great Grandfather ?*

Mrs Shanks: *Dad's mother's father had a private lending library in Kirkcaldy; Burt's Lending Library. We still have old books from it.*

JB: *A Private lending Library?*

Mrs Shanks: *Oh yes...that's how people educated themselves-they knew that they had to read to get on.*

There is a connection between this and Thomas Carlyle. Of course, he has a connection with Fife anyway, but he used to come and stay with my mother-in-laws father, who was a farmer. He used to send word when he was arriving in Fife and they used to give him a donkey to ride on. He used to ride into the country on it; presumably to get inspiration. Of course, he sent them a copy of every book he wrote - to my great grandfather - Thomson......But I'm a bit hazy about that one. The books aren't here unfortunately, they're on the Thomson side. They keep them in a big kist, I believe; a big wooden box. I don't think anyone ever read them- they would say "Oh No. Not anither one !" and chuck it in the box !

I have a few old Carlyle's..old books from my Father. It was something I was very conscious of, he had so many books...thousands, literally.

JB: *Did any come from your fathers library?*

Municipal Election
WARD III.

MEN AND WOMEN ELECTORS.

Lenin's Message to the Communists:--

"Use the Municipal Machine from within to smash up the present System of Society."

DON'T BE MISLED.
VOTE THUS:

Blyth, And., Senior, Loughb'h Road, Linen Manufacturer.		**X**
Brodie, Robt., Loughborough Road, Engineer.		**X**
BRYCE, WM., 76 Harriet Street, Miner.		
CLARK, JAMES, 165 Overton Road, Miner.		
M'CORMACK, J. D., 25 Dysart Rd., Hardwarem'n		
Napier, Hy., Senior, Bandon Avenue, Engineer.		**X**
WESTWOOD, J. 52 Pottery St., Political Organiser		

Printed and Published by The Fifeshire Advertiser Ltd., 130 High Street, Kirkcaldy.

Mrs Shanks : *No..I don't think so, no...he was a great collector of first editions, and of course John Buchan... He was at Kirkcaldy for a time. His father was a minister at Pathhead and my father went to the same primary school.*

I have masses of old photographs of old worthies from Kirkcaldy....going back a hundred years. It makes me think, why do people never put information on the back of old photographs ? So do start now! For your family....names and dates !!

My Mother was pupil at the Wemyss School of Needlework.. Her name was Nancy Grieve.

There was some connection between the Wemyss family and my Mother but she never told us what it was. Basically, we don't know who she was or where she came from. We have a photo of her and Admiral Wemyss and a beautiful Lady in Paris. I always like to imagine that that was her Father...but we'll never know.

JB: *That's very intriguing indeed! And very frustrating....*

Mrs Shanks: *Yes. We were far too well brought up to ask questions and she never told us, but there was definitely some connection between her and the Wemyss'. She had books with the fly-leaf torn out and you can just make out Queen Alexanda's signature....and RL Stevenson's 'Verses for Children'... the fly-leaf of that has been torn out as well...we'll never know....*

When my mother died we didn't know where she'd been born or anything.
We got her birth certificate and it said she had been born in Bradfield, in England. She was incredibly elegant....wonderful hands...none of her three daughters inherited it!
But she was someone very special. She was brought up by the gardener.
They educated her. She was given to them as a babe. That was one thing she did used to say:

"These people are not my father and mother!"

Embroidery Pattern from Wemyss School of Needlework

Alan Jennings, Cupar.

My Dad, John C Jennings, worked for the GPO and later BT. He came up to Scotland in the 1970's and took a post at Dundee, retiring in 1983.

He doesn't speak much about his work, but the little said sounds very interesting:

The area he covered included Tayside, Fife and stretched into Grampian and over to Strathclyde. As an engineering manager, his responsibility was to ensure proper and effective telephone communications as a public service. This meant dealing with a ground staff of perhaps 200-300 and ensuring their jobs were done well.

On one occasion he was called out to attend a fault at Craigowl in the winter and the only way to reach the station was on a snowcat.

Also, there was a government listening station (something to do with national security), near Cupar which was his responsibility to maintain.

Once, there was a Perthshire customer who had a problem so severe that he found out our home telephone number and got my Dad to see to it personally.

One winter, the main electric line that runs up the A9 was cut by lightening and this had the effect of a power surge transmitted to a local sub-station next to an exchange Dad was inspecting. Late in the evening he saw it glowing blue in the dark!

There doesn't seem to be much in the way of recognition for ordinary folk doing a very good job of work and he certainly doesn't look for accolades. Nevertheless, without constant attention and hard work, things most of us take for granted would come to a halt quick as an eye blink.

Mrs Mary Douglas, Kinghorn.

20 Minutes of Hell

In August 1930, at 2pm on a sunny afternoon, three laddies were fishing for flounders 200 yards of the Carlin Head in Kinghorn Bay. The beach was crowded, the sea quiet, the scene happy.

Archie Smith, 14 years old from Kinghorn, Stuart Galloway and Tommy Otter, both 16 years old, from Edinburgh, sat contented in the 12 foot rowing boat 'Rose Marie'. Archie was sitting on the anchor chain in the bow, Stuart in the stern and Tommy on the middle seat.

The sky clouded over from the west, suddenly darkening ominously and the heavens opened up in a deluge of rain. Archie pulled up the anchor, then turned to put in a rowlock and oar. A sharp hiss - lightning struck - and poor Tommy was killed outright, Archie was burned on his left side. The boat was holed, with the elbows each side of the centre seat split. The boat tipped vertically bow first, plunging Archie with his left side paralysed, into the sea, followed by the charred remains of Tommy - only recognisable by his shoes. Stuart, not physically harmed, hung onto the stern for grim death.

Archie went down twice, trying to grasp the timbers of the boat with his right hand. As he surfaced for the third time, Stuart Galloway clamped his legs around Archie and held on.

39

Another boat, with Scouts on board, came alongside, pulled them to safety and rowed them to shore. The tragic sight of Tommy's mother, waist deep in water, skirt floating, arms outstretched, crying " where's Tommy?" "Where's my Tommy?" seared into their memory as they were helped onto the beach.

The sun was now shining again.

My Uncle Archie, now aged 82 years, still lives on the bay in Kinghorn. Tommy Otter rests in Kinghorn Cemetery and Stuart Galloway's whereabouts are unknown.

FALKLaND

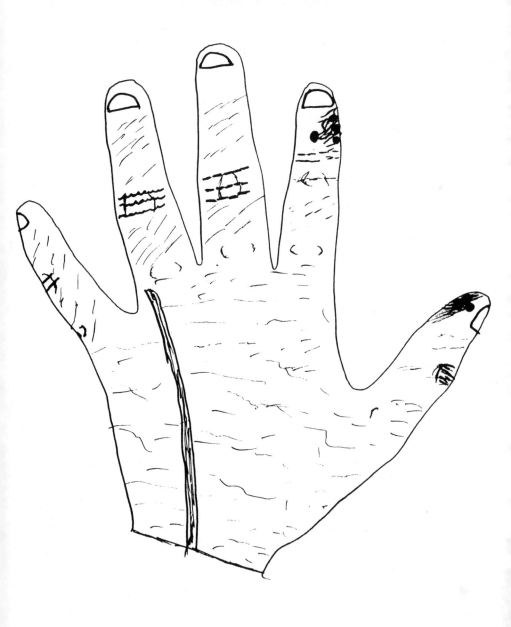

Heather Binnie (Kirkcaldy North)

Sean Binnie was wanting to watch his TV in his room, but he didn't have a plug on his TV so he tried to put the wire in the socket on the wall and suddenly he got the shock of his life as he was being electrocuted. His friend Ryan who was with him realised that his best friend Sean was being electrocuted, he quickly pulled the wire away from the socket.

Sean didn't die but he had badly burnt fingers. He was too scarred to go through to his mum so he and Ryan put lots of plasters on his hand. After an hour he went for his tea, when his mum Jan noticed he had plasters on his fingers, then she asked what had happened. Sean told her and took the plasters off his hands. Jan quickly, as fast as she could put her coat on and took him to the hospital. The doctor said he was fine and he got a bandage on his hand. It healed up in the matter of two months. He got front page in the Fife Free Press and Tenth Page in the Daily Record, his hand had healed up now but he still regrets what he's done.

44

45

Kirsten Burns (Collydean)

My Mum is my special person. She helps to look after an elderly neighbour who is really getting confused. My Mum makes sure she doesn't go out on her own as she is getting really wobbly on her feet.

On Friday she helps her into a taxi to go to a club. My Mum is really kind by helping our neighbour. I don't think that the old lady would stay in her house. I am really proud of my Mum and I am happy that she is looking after the lady while her daughter is at work. I am really proud of my Mum.

Jenny (Falkland)

My mum is very special because she reads me stories and makes me lunch and puts me to bed. I love my mum a lot. My mummy takes me for long walks and to different countries. She takes me to special towns and cities.

BREAD
CURRY.
SAUCE.
ICE LOLLIES
CIDER
WINE.
TOBACCO.
C/PAPERS
D/FOOD

Sammy Braid (Kirkcaldy North)

My brother is special in ways that he has problems. He fell off a tree swing and hurt his elbow. He had to get rushed to casualty and they told my mum that they could not do anything with it and they had to send him to Sick Kids in Edinburgh. They operated on him and they took a vein out of his arm, he was in the hospital for three months. He had to keep his arm in the air, something was holding his arm up, I think it would be tiring. When he got home he had to keep it in a splinter, he went to physio every month, but now he goes every year. He has another problem. I don't know what it is called but it is a long word. He bruises easily, like if you punch him soft, he will bruise. He is football crazy, he is fanatic about Dunfermline I think he likes Dunfermline because my grandad used to play for them. When one of the players died, I don't know his name, he went to Dunfermline and put his football shirt down on his grave and he put his scarf down too. He used to be the school goalie, he was the best goalie in the school. He only let 13 goals in the whole the time he was the goalie.

Lee Jamieson (Collydean)

My special heroes are my best friend's foster parents who fostered six children. Their names are Peter, who is 12 years old, David, who is 15 years old, Allan, who is 14 years old, Niall, who is 4 years old, Joe, who is two years old and Michael, who is 17 years old. Peter is my best friend. Their foster parents are called Dave and Agnes who are very kind and generous. I think they have a lot of courage to foster six children. They even let me come to lunch and dinner several times a week. To me they are true heroes. Sometimes when I stay at their house, I feel like they are fostering me.

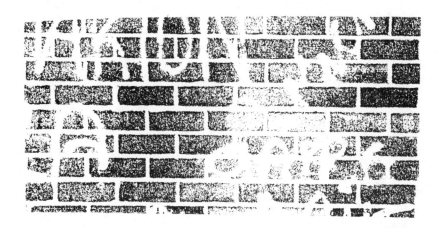

Thomas Murphy. Paratrooper.
Home town. Kelty. Fife.

Involved in the battle of Arnheim during the WW2.
Captured by Germans, he was held in a POW camp
until his escape. Taken in by a family in Holland, he
stayed for a considerable time until he was able to
make the journey back to his homeland. An address
he left in a chest of drawers was discovered years
later by a member of the family who had
safeguarded him and a reunion took place. On his
return home from the war, Thomas had received no
answer from his Mother's house and traced her to
the local co-op where he found out he had been
listed as dead in the list of war deceased.

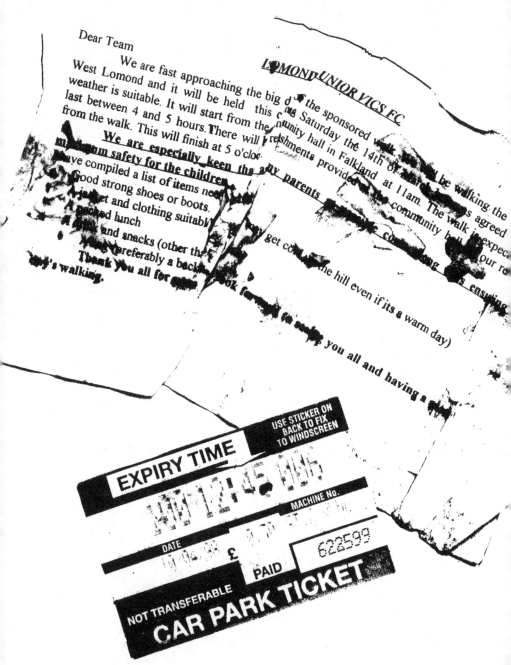

Mr James Mill. Dovecot Farm, Falkland.

I am writing about my father, Mr W. P. Mill, who at the time stayed in R****** Lodge in Ladybank, in 1909. He rescued a boy from drowning in the river Eden, which runs between Ladybank and King's Kettle, and was awarded a silver engraved watch and scroll from the Carnegie Hero Fund. Shortly after this he joined the army when the first world war broke out, as he had not yet met my mother. She was also in the army, the WAC's, whose present day name would be the ATS. After the war he married in 1920 and I was born in 1922. He served in Africa and France, but later my mother and him......well, he joined the army again in 1939, in the Military Police and my mother joined the ambulance service. I joined the Fife and Forfar Yeomanry in 1938 and was called up in September 1939. I landed   on the beaches of Normandy with the 1st Northamptonshire Yeomanry and served with them throughout the war in France and Germany until I was demobilised. I returned to the railway, where I had worked before, at Ladybank. My Great Grandfather, Mr Andrew Mill, had been the first signalman at Ladybank, when the railway was first put through. My father and Grandfather were also on the Ladybank railway, so was my Uncle and so was I. There were many James Mill's. James Mill was my Uncle, my son is called William Mill and his son is called James Mill. My Grandmother died at Ladybank a few years ago aged 102. My father died a few years ago and my mother too. I also went with the 1st Northants to the Ardennes and fought through Holland and Germany ending up at Herman Goering's works near Hanover. That's all I can remember just now.

Paul Fleming (Sinclairtown)

I'm sad because my uncle went to Germany to live because he joined the army and I've never seen him since last summer.(I hope he comes back one day).

Aaron (Falkland)

I like my cousin because he goes to the Circus. He goes on a unicycle and does tricks and is juggling at the same time. And he puts face paint on and he puts funny shoes on and funny clothes.

Nicholas (Falkland)

My Grandad is a very good man. He is never strict. My Gran is dede. He is sad, but he is giving me all the love. I fink he spoils me a lot.

Catriona (Falkland)

I once had a friend called Jennifer. I met her on holiday in Spain. When we got there we went to the beach. I did not know her at all then. I just went over to her and asked her to play frisbee. She said yes and while we played we asked each other questions, like what is your name? How old are you? Soon, we got to know each other very well indeed. I went to her house every day and sometimes she came to mine. One day, she had to leave. We said goodbye, but not before she had given me her address. When we went back to Scotland I wrote to her and she wrote to me. Then I forgot to write back. Then I remembered but no reply ever came. I am still waiting for the reply if it ever comes. She might not remember me because I was only five when it happened.

jam
marmalade
t.bags
milk.
soup that I like. ( )
diluting juice blackcurant
ice cream. lchoclies.
tea bags.

Mrs Abernethy

Joshua. (Sinclairtown)

My dads War

My dAdS War. My DAdrunclr grandAd thot 5000 zolos mydAds Best frend got Killt my dad climd on to th CAMP roof r a zolo folodhir my dAd grabd one end of the gun the zolo grabd the other end and my dAd Kicd the zolo down on to a spick my grarda got shot on the leg at nitht the zolos enveded our campat nitht agen.

56

Pauline Seath (Collydean)

My special person is my Great Gran. She pulled someone out from a burning car. Then she 'phoned the police and an ambulance and caught the person who put the car on fire. She was nineteen and she was pregnant. She also survived a car crash at twenty- one. The car crashed into a huge lorry and the only injury she had was a broken arm and leg. She also lost a husband in the war and the husband she has now has been married to her for sixty years.
She was a nurse in World War Two and she has seen a lot of dead bodies and that was when her first husband died. She has saved over fifty people and was just about killed wrapping up someone's arm. Lots of her friends died in the war and she pulled through the depression and sadness with difficulty, but she did it.

Now, my Great Gran is very loving and shows she loves my whole family. I am proud of her and she is proud of herself. Of all she has been through she can still go on holidays and wander around the shops of Dundee and Fife with ease. She is now Eighty-four and I think she will live ten more years at least.

John Stewart. (Aberhill School. MAD Kids Club)

A special person to me is my mum. She cares for me and helps me do things for school. When my dad got a new job in England and we wouldn't see him a lot she was able to cope with me and my two brothers. She has to cook, wash and iron for us and we try to help her the best we can. It makes it harder for her because she is a teacher and she also has her school work.

My mam by John Stewart.

Charlene Wallace (Kirkcaldy North)

My special person is Mr Clark my violin teacher he has a little girl but I do not know her name. If you are a very very good pupil he gives you presents I've got about four already. He is a very nice man and I bet his child is very glad that he is her dad. He teaches other schools like Viewforth. He thinks I am really getting on with my violin. I've got a certificate from 1 of my concerts. My headteacher says "Oh Charlene, you are representing the school" and I told my mum and she said I am really proud of you. I have done 4 concerts already. My violin teacher's wife plays the violin too. Mr Clark plays with a string band they got the band name from them all playing violins and cellos because they have got strings. Mr Clarks wife plays in the band too. I don't know if their child plays the violin or not but I think she does. I had a girl partner for the violin but she quit. So I got another partner and he is called Scott, he is very funny. Mrs Clark is very proud of me and so is my mum.

Violin is super

Violin is what I play,
I practice it every day,
Oh what a lovely lovely sound,
Lovely, lovely sound that I found,
I'm glad I got chosen to play,
Now that is what I do all day.

59

Steven by Jenna (Falkland Primary School)

Lee Logie (East Wemyss)

My friend Richard saved me once. I was going to fall off a pier into the water. He was really quick. He grabbed my hand.

I saved Richard twice. He was falling off a shed and he landed on my legs.

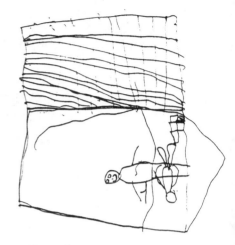

Kirsten McLaughlin (East Wemyss)

My Mum is the best of the rest. She is nice and good and properly the best mum in the world.
She is best because she lets do me anything I want and she cares for me. She also gives me lots of good sweets. When I don't feel well she looks after me. My mum helps me with my homework. She is more like my best friend than my mum.
She has short hair and works in a shop at McDuff in East Wemyss. That's why I like my mum.

Craig Watson (East Wemyss)

I like Lee Logie and Steven Parker because they are protecting me when I am going to get battered because Steven is my pal and Lee is my cousin and we are good cousins and Lee always calls me by and all the time in his house he calls me Barbie and I wear a Barbie skirt. That is what Lee says and I always batter him because he is annoying and he runs away ben his sisters room and ben the kitchen.

Robyn Smart (East Wemyss)

My best friend is Jade Hughes. We have been friends for four years. This is how we became friends. When I first began school I had nobody to play with at playtime but she came up to me and asked if I would play with her so I said "Yes". We are still friends now. We have broken up before, but we never last a day without each other. I sometimes go and play with other people and she gets upset about it and that is how we break up. When I go up to her house we go for walks. The best place we go is The Den. The Den is made of wood and when we grow up we are hoping to live beside each other.

Rebecca Peebles (East Wemyss)

I like my friend Stephen. He is 8 months old. He is very special to me. He sometimes comes to stay with me at my aunties house for all the night. He has got some blond hair and blue eyes. His birthday is on the 5th of October. He can't walk yet, but he's getting there. He is very cute. His mum is called Yvonne.

Denise Bell drew Sandra (Kirkaldy North)

Lynn Smith (Collydean)

My Gran is the best in my life because she helps people that is sick. My Gran also helps to raise money for charity. She holds sales in her garden for all different causes. She always takes me to charity shops and she is always giving up her spare time to raise money. Her friends held a sale with raffle tickets, jewellery and much more. My Gran took me and I was helping. There was food as well. A Man had made German soup that was 20p for a big bowl. We raised about £150 altogether and it all went to Special Needs. And my Gran does anything for her friends.......

Shaun Greig   (Collydean)

My hero is my uncle, Andy Greig who plays with instruments. He mostly plays the accordion. He also does Scottish country dancing with schools. He started when he was sixteen and he's now in his fifties. Just a few months ago he became famous with a few of his mates. He did a few tunes and then just became famous. He has made a lot of money by playing the accordion.

Sarah McCollie (Collydean

My hero would have to be my Dad because one night we were going to the fish and chip shop for the tea when we saw a light that flashed very quickly then a bang.

After the bang there was nothing.

We saw that a car had spun and gone in the ditch beside the road. One of the boys had got their arm caught round the seat belt so my dad helped to take his arm out, then he 'phoned for the Police. When the Police came me and my Dad went for our fish and chips.

Gemma Watson (Sinclairtown)

My Grandad plays for Aberdeen and he scored a great goal. He tackled a Raith Rovers player and he fell down and hurt his leg. It was painful but he wasn't crying.

I like my grandad because he is funny, too. My grandad laughs loud. I like it when my Grandad laughs because he makes me laugh too. My grandad makes everybody laugh.

Gordon Vimpany (Collydean)

I have very bad hay-fever and I didn't have any medication for a while, but my mum saw how bad it was. My eyes were popping out their sockets because they were very itchy and my nose was sometimes so runny that it would fill up the Pacific Ocean. Sometimes it is so blocked up that if my nose was a tap it would be impossible to get water out.

My Superhero is my Mum because she got me my hay-fever tablets and stopped me from waking up at night swimming in what comes out of my nose.

James Mack   (Kirkcaldy North)

My self is my hero and I want to be a football player. If I don't get to be a football player I will be an artist and I will write about people who is heroes and I used to be in the school football team but I was taken out because I will be in it next year.

David Brand (Kirkcaldy North)

My Dad was a goalkeeper for the Raith Rovers supporters club and the Fife Stars. His name is George. In one of the games Coventry's manager came to watch him and thought he was good. They said if he was the same for another three matches he would get a trial to be Coventry's goalie but on the fourth game he ripped his knee ligaments and was rushed to hospital.   And he needed an operation and he needed fisio, feripy every week. Nowadays he is a tour driver, he works alone and is in a video that Glamis Castle made.

68

**Emma Victoria Kirby. Portrait of David Shaw.
(Collydean)**

Lauren Stewart (Collydean)

When I was very young - I might not even have been born- my Dad swam under the Forth Road Bridge. My brother who is a few years older than me comes up in the loft with me sometimes to look for a paper bit which my Dad cut out to keep. We once found it then my Dad put it away again, so we are still looking for it.

Christopher Mutter (Collydean)

My sister is a professional dancer and she is really good. She started dancing at the age of eight. She went to Janet Malcolm dancers school and still does. She would like to go to dance college and be a dancer on cruise ships. We'll be very pleased if she does because all she does is dance.

Lee-Ann, my sister (who is about thirty years old), would like to be a **dance teacher like Janet, Lee-Ann's teacher. There is another girl, Lauren Copland, who likes what Lee-Ann is going to do and that's what she would like to do. Lauren is very keen and is only twelve years old.**

One day I hope this will all happen, but we will have to build another room because she has already got 356 medals, most of which are for first place.

.adybank draw

he draw for the Open Scratch competition at Lad...
day is:
712 and 1154 — D. Paton, Dunn...
3 and 1200 — A. Gardiner,
4 and 1206 — K. Whiteha
ybank; 0730 and 1212 — R.
ybank; 07.36 and 1218 —
.allum, St Andrews; 0742 and
McCue, Ladybank; 0748 and 12
. Grant, Ladybank; 0754 and 12
ludie, Ladybank.
800 and 1242 — A. Paterson
rnton; 0806 and 1248 — D. A. T... ...all, K. Gardiner,
itrose; 0812 and 1254 — J. Dun ..., Balbirnie, M. Feeney,
vnfield; 0818 and 1300 — M. Taylor, Balbirnie, C. V.
aldson, Downfield; 0824 and 1306 — R. Bissett, Brechin, P.
iningham, Downfield; 0836 and 1318 — B. Mason,
nikiker Park, Ryan Bremner, Glenrothes; 0842 and 1324 —
Mason, Dunnikier Park, G. McNab, Leven Thistle; 0848 and
1 — D. G. Gatherum, Ladybank, S   mmell, Uphall; 0854
1336 — P Stewart, Ladybank   Merchants.
100 and 1342 — B. Her   mbar
8 and 1348 —
.thaven; n
.thau

● Kirkcaldy
team wins Fife
Netball League

Carnegie
starlets
go Dutch

FIVE members
Carnegie Judo Club were
hoping to prove a handful
when they set off for an
international competition
in Holland this week.

TEAMS

LADY
GOLFERS!

Glenwood's
netball girls
urt success

Three off
in cup win

GLENROTHES .. 2
KELTY HEARTS .. 1

GLENS shocked the
new champio...

Falkland too stro

GLENROTHES
Juniors bring
the curtain down
on the John Fyfe
League season
t o n i g h t
(Thursday) with
proof that
progress has

Alastair

Fife found portraits: **Kirkcaldy**

Lenville Burn (Collydean)

My special person is my Mum, she always takes me to places and plays with me. I think she sets a good example. I look up to her even if I get a row for being bad. She always works hard and always offers encouragement.

I try to be kind to her, so I help her do the shopping and things around the house. When she is out the house it is hectic. Even though she is pregnant she always handles everything and looks after me, my two brothers, my sister and my Dad. I can tell her anything. I can always rely on her. If I ask for help I can get it from her.

Me and my dad try to help her when she is tired. When she comes back from night shift she still stays up for a while to make us breakfast. Even when she feels ill, I know what to do because she taught me. She is my hero.

Ryan Doig (East Wemyss)

My dad is a hero because when he was little he saved animals because stupid boys set fire to the barn. The animals were saved because my dad and grandad were brave enough to save them. I do not know if the boys got a row or not. I think my dad is a super animal hero. I love him very much. I think he is totally a hero because of it and he had to take all the balls.

My Dad is my friend.

My best friend Allan

Once when I came to East Wemyss Primary School, Allan kept me from getting hit. He always plays with me and lends me his pencil. We've been friends for three years and still are, yet we've had some fall outs but not major. He learns me moves and he is huge.

Ryan Doig   east Wyms Primary   Age 8

My dad is a Hero because when he was little he
saved animals in The barn because stupid boys
set Fire to The barn. The animals were saved becaus
my Bdad and Grandad were brave enough to save Them, I
Do notno if The boys got a row or not I Think my Dad
is a Super animal Hero, I Love Him very much

I Think He is toetaly a Hero because of it
and He Had to take all THe balse

My Dad is my Frend.

My best Freand alLN

once when I came to east
wyems primary scool Allan kept me From geting
Hit. He always plays whith me and lets me His pesrt
we've been freand For Three years andstill are yet
we've Had some Fall outs but not magere and Lear.
me moves and He is Huge Hill
ya

Amy Edmondson. (Sinclairtown)

My Dad in Preston used to be with my Mum. By the time Carolyn was born (My big sister) my Dad had lost two people in his family. First he lost his sister Julie and then he lost his Dad. He went out to the ice-cream van and when he came back he sat down to eat his ice-cream but he took a heart attack so he didn't get to eat his ice-cream. So that's why I think he's so special and so brave-to go through with all those deaths and still have me !

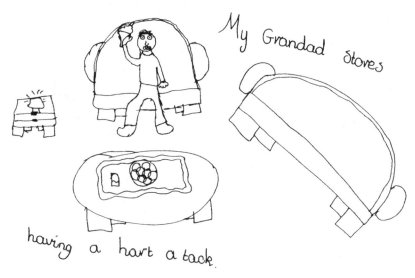

My Grandad Stoves

having a hart a tack.

Kevin Fong (Kirkcaldy North)

One day my friend Mohammed saved a cats life. He was playing in his garden and he saw a cat on the road and a car coming. The cat was lying down and the cat got up and the car ran over it's leg. Mohammed seen it and he ran and got his mum to take the cat to the hospital.   The doctor told Mohammed and his mum that the cat will be all right but the cat has three legs. The driver went off when it happened.   Mohammed didn't find it's master so he got to keep the cat.

78

Amy E. by Paul Woods (Sinclairtown Primary)

Callum Law. (Collydean)

My hero is my Uncle Christopher Stevenson, who survived a tragedy like a real fighter. It was winter time and my Uncle had been meaning to go on a parachute jump for ages and he thought this time would be perfect.
So, in the afternoon the airplane was cruising at 30,000 feet and he was going to jump onto Falkland Hill. So he jumped and when he was just about going to press the parachute button he pulled the release cord and he plunged 14,750 feet to certain doom. But he fell into 15 feet of heavy snow. He had to stay in hospital for eight weeks, but he survived.

My Mum

Joan Burchill (Collydean)

My special person is my Mom. She helped someone who fell out of a parachute. She checked if the man was OK, then she went for help. She came back two minutes later with an ambulance. The man wasn't badly injured. He had just broke his legs...and his left arm. The man got took to Kirkcaldy Hospital after jumping Falkland Hill. The man was out of hospital in two weeks.

Fife found portraits: **Methil**

Heather Davie *(East Wemyss)*

When I broke up for Easter holidays, Laura, one of my best friends came up for me and we went for Alan and we played on the swings. John- Paul and Stuart came to the park and Stuart went on the back of my swing then he jumped off. Then I fell off and I was knocked out. Laura and Alan carried me up to Alan's house and his dad took me up the road. Then I went to hospital and I had to stay in overnight. If it wasn't for Laura and Alan it would have been worse.

Rena S. (East Wemyss)

My Gran and Grandad are special to me. They are getting on a bit. They are getting me a Celtic ring. I went to Gran's house and she bought me a Celtic necklace as well. I am going to watch the football match between Scotland and Norway tonight and I will get my tea at my Gran's and a cup of coffee.

**Katrina Hynes. Portrait of Mrs McQuillan
(Kirkcaldy North)**

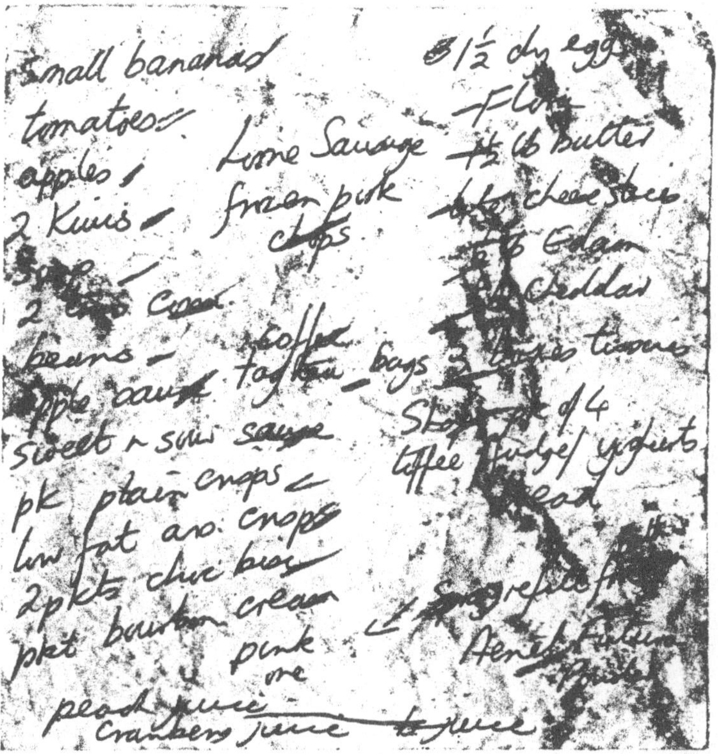

small bananas
tomatoes
apples
2 Kiwis
2 ... cream
beans
apple sauce
sweet & sour sauce
pk plain crisps
low fat ass. crisps
2pkts choc bics
pkt bourbon cream
pink
peach juice
Cranberry juice juice

Lorne Sausage
frozen pork chops
coffee
tea bags

3 1/2 dz eggs
Flour
1/2 lb butter
cheese slices
Edam
Cheddar
3 boxes tissues
pk of 4 toffee fudge yoghurts
bread
refill

Kay Giles (Collydean)

My Grandad takes me everywhere. He works a lot but he tries to take me out when he can. His dog died and he was sad. I gave him a card. He lives in Dunfermline. When I stay he takes me everywhere and he buys me lots of things. He is very kind to me. He makes sawdust. He gives my mum sawdust for my animals. He helps me a lot and is very nice to me so I give him lots of presents. I give him lots of things for his room for him to look at. Then his room looks nice from all the things I've given him. He is kind and likes me. So, that's my Grandad.....and a kind, loving Grandad....

Scott Jefferson (Collydean)

One day last year my dad's friend Steve saved me from drowning in a swimming pool in England. I went off a diving board and landed on my belly and was sinking. I reached the surface a couple of times and I was kicking and thrashing at the water. Steve saw me and rescued me from drowning. That is why Steve is my hero. He is also my hero for other things. I could have picked anyone in my family because they are all very special to me.

David Montgomerie (Collydean)

One day last year my mum saved my gran from dying. Then, when gran was better she went back up to her house in Wilmington Drive. A couple of months later she took ill again and my Mum brought her back to my house and nursed her for several months.
My two aunties helped my mum but it wasn't enough. My gran died.

Kirsten Dunnett.
Portrait of Kay Giles.

Ashley Mitchell (Collydean)

One night last year, just before I went to bed I got my Rat Delboy out, played with him for ten minutes then put him back. I didn't realise that I'd left his cage open. I cuddled up in my bed and I was so tired that I dropped off in about ten minutes. In the night I was aware of a loud scraping sound at my bedroom door. I quickly jumped out of bed to see what it was. It was Delboy, shaking like mad. I picked him up and cuddled him. It was then I discovered the smell of gas. I ran downstairs and felt the door. It was hot. I ran back upstairs and shouted that their was a fire. My Mum and Dad got up and ran down the stairs, then they 'phoned the Fire Brigade. They arrived 15 minutes later, by which time all of my family were standing in the garden. I suddenly realised that I had left Delboy upstairs after he had just saved our family, so I ran into the house and up the stairs. Of course, I did get a few burns, but I grabbed Delboy and got out of the house.

When the fire was put out we had to move in with my Gran for a month while the house was getting fixed. So, after all that, it was my rat that saved all our lives. He is my Hero.

Morgan Smith (Sinclairtown)

My Gran and Grandad are called Daphne and James McEwan. They were in the Second World War. My Gran was a nurse and my Grandad was an army pilot. When my Gran was a nurse she helped a man that was shot three times and he almost died but she got all three bullets out just in time. Then she met my Grandad when he was injured by the blaze of the bomb. When I was three she died of a heart attack.

Kirsten Dunnett. (Collydean)

I'm writing about my two friends Michelle Shields and Michelle Kirbitson. I've chosen them because they are always there for me. I feel so better once I've told them my problems and worries.

For instance there was this boy called Stuart. He was in our class. Unfortunately he died. All the girls were crying. I would like to thank them for comforting me and being there.

There are also two other heroes. Stuart's mum and dad. Once Stuart died, his mum and dad gave parts of his body away to people that need it and they saved lives.

Debbie Smith. (Collydean)

My grandmother (Ina Smith) is very special to me because she helped a little bird get free from a little bush. She got it out and put it on top of a shed so she could put it in a box but it tried to fly away and landed in her next door neighbours garden. It's mother flew past and tried to help it but unfortunately did not succeed.

Simon Barlow. (Collydean)

My uncle Charles did a sponsored walk for 10 miles. He started at Newport he went across the Tay Bridge for 5 miles and 5 miles back across the Tay Bridge. Then he stayed at home of a week in his bed.

Kay Giles. Portrait of Kirsten Dunnett.

My grandads bedroom.

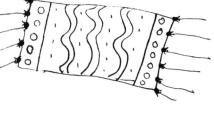

The BIGGEST card For the best Groendad.

morror

Kay Giles, collydean.

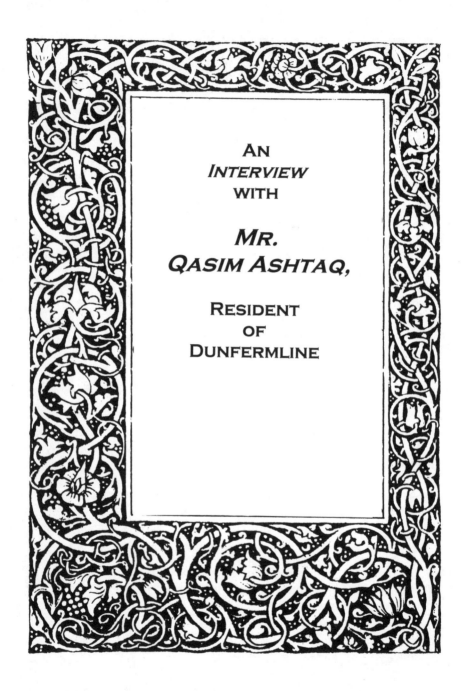

AN
INTERVIEW
WITH

MR.
QASIM ASHTAQ,

RESIDENT
OF
DUNFERMLINE

Interview with Qasim Ashtaq. Feb. 1998

JB. *Qasim, where were you born and how old are you?*

Qasim. *In Falkirk. Falkirk hospital. I'm fifteen years old.*

JB. What about your family ?

Qasim. *Well....originally they are from Pakistan - Sahiwal- When the British had it, it was called Montgomery. It's in the east.*

JB. When did they come to Scotland ?

Qasim. *I dunno. Before I was born. My Dad was born in Bristol. He worked as an engineer on cars.*

JB. Did he train as an engineer in Pakistan?

Qasim. *No, like I said...he was born in Bristol, so he was starting everything from there.*

JB. What about your mum?

Qasim. *She's from Sahiwal.*

JB. So...you go to school here in Dunfermline.

Qasim. *Aye. Queen Anne High School. I'm just about to do my standard grades in May. I'm revising like mad!*

JB. I met you last month for the first time in the Spice of Life Restaurant here in Dunfermline. How long have you worked there?

Qasim. *For two years. At first I was a Pizza chef, then a Kebab chef then it changed hands and I became a waiter.*

JB. *I must say I thought the food was very good in there. The best I've had in Scotland!*

Qasim. *Aye...there's a lot of good ones in Glasgow as well...*

JB. *So You're a waiter now... a rather chatty, friendly waiter!-Do you always spend so much time chatting to customers or was I especially privileged ?*

Qasim. *Aye! Because I like talking to all of them. It's better if you do, because...I like to get to know the customers. Know if they enjoyed the food. If they come regularly you'll know who they are and what to expect.*

JB. *Do you get a lot of regulars ?*

Qasim. *Oh yes. Like last night- there's a couple who come from Kincardine. They haven't been for three weeks, but they usually come every week. They had been to see their son in Mull, I think. Where Nick Nairn is made. Do you watch that programme? He's a Chef. A Scottish TV chef.*

JB. *Are you fond of cooking Then?*

Qasim. *No!*

JB. *How often do you work in the restaurant? Do you have any family connection with the owner?*

Qasim. *Well - my mother knows the owner's sister. I work there two days a week. Friday night and Saturday. I don't want to stay in the catering trade, 'though...I'ts not enough for me.*

96

JB. *So - What do you want to do when you leave school.*

Qasim. *I want to be an Artist! Aye - Art and Design.*

JB. *That's what I did; I went to Art School for four years. Are you doing Art at school?*

Qasim. *Aye. I do...I enjoy it.*

JB. *Tell me about your school. Do you think it's any good ?*

Qasim. *It is, yeah. It's one of the best schools in Dunfermline, probably. It's a public (state) school. You know, anyone can go there. You don't need money. It's a good school, 'though.*

JB. *What are the other schools in Dunfermline like?*

Qasim. *I dunno. You can't say, cos you've not been to them. You can only base your opinion on what you've seen.*

JB. *Have you ever been bullied?*

Qasim. *No. There's no problem. Not really, no.*

JB. *Is there a big ethnic community in Dunfermline?*

Qasim. *Not really. There's about twelve in my school, out of about 1000- odd pupils.*

JB. *Are there any gangs in your school ?*

Qasim. *Not really. Well, their might be gangs but they're not in the open. They've not been exposed. No-ones got the idea, like 'we're a gang' - Dunfermline is a gang - they'll fight kids from Cowdenbeath - real stupid things like that. You go to an under 18's disco and you'll see a big group of them outside*

Gary Pearson drew Christopher McKellar

and a big group of Cowdenbeath or Kircaldy and all big scraps happen.

JB. What about drugs. Is there a noticeable problem ?

Qasim. There is, yes. You can tell who's on drugs easily, though. There are boys in our class. Have you seen the weed sign? They have that all over their folders. It's pretty obvious. You can tell.

JB. Do you have drugs awareness lessons at school?

Qasim. No. They say 'Drugs is Bad', and that's about it.

JB. What other languages, apart from English, can you speak?

Qasim. Punjabi. It's my first language. Aye...English comes second.

JB. What do you feel that you are? If, say, you had the chance to play international cricket or football, for instance, would you choose Scotland or Pakistan?

Qasim. Scotland. Because if you're born there, you'd say Pakistan, but if you are born here you'd have to say Scotland.

JB. So, do you feel very Scottish ?

Qasim. Aye....I do.

JB. And do you like sport? Is there a chance of you representing your country at football ?

Qasim. Ha ha ha. I don't know about that. I do like sport, though...Basketball, Cricket, Football and Badminton. I don't play in any teams, though...I've no time at the minute.

JB. So..apart from working and school, what do you do in your spare time ?

Qasim. *Here in Fife ? Nothing much. When I was ten, we used to go over the fields and that on our bikes. Or play football in someone's back yard or in the street, and that's about it. There's not enough things to do here, compared to like, Glasgow. They don't even have a decent cinema here. There is one, up in Eastport, but it's pretty small. You can go ten pin bowling, but that's down in Rosyth. It ought to be here! We don't have any modern facilities for kids here. I think that's right enough. I think bringing modernism into an old town.......you've got a church and an abbey and if you put a lot of skyscrapers in....I know, to some extent it's alright but....especially if you've got, say, new companies coming into Dunfermline, like Hyundai and that...They invest money and then they...you've probably heard about Hyundai?.....It's not open anymore. It's stupid. To spend so much money and then...they went bust.*

JB. *Is there anyone in your family who you particularly admire?*

Qasim. *I admire my uncles, who own a nightclub here in Dunfermline. I think they worked really hard when they were young to get the money together. They had a restaurant and my dad used to work there as well. He runs a restaurant in Perth, now.*

JB. **Retailing and catering are very common professions amongst the Asian community in Britain. I remember when you could only get fish and chips and shops shut at 5.30 every night. They filled a huge market gap, didn't they. Now every town in the country has its shops staying open and its ethnic restaurants. Our whole attitude to shopping and eating has been changed thanks largely to the Asian community.**

Qasim. *Yes, that's true, but I don't really like the idea of all the Indian and Chinese restaurants. I don't think it's right. Each town should just have the one Indian, one chip shop.*

JB. *Is the food you serve the same as you eat at home ?*

Qasim. *Not really, no. It's about 10% the same. The restaurants serve food from lots of different areas like Persia and Turkey.*

JB. **Do you change what's on the menu according to what you think people will eat in a certain area ?**

Qasim. *No, not really. You take a risk at that point.*

JB. **Do people ever complain that, for instance, this isn't a Biryani. I had one in Huddersfield last week and it was completely different ?**

Qasim. *Yeah!. We've had that one. But...every restaurant is different, really.*

JB. People with Pakistani or Indian backgrounds tend to be a bit stereotyped by the catering trade, I find. You know, people automatically presume that you must own or work in a restaurant...

Qasim. *Yes, it is a problem. Like I said, I want to back away from it. That's why I want to be an artist.*

JB. Do you think you'll stay in Scotland?

Qasim. *No. I want to move away. I want to go to America. I've got cousins out there. In San Francisco. I've no been there yet, but I want to go.*

JB. A surprising amount of people of your age in Scotland have said that to me.

Qasim. *Aye. America is where everything is. But I don't like Americans. I think they're stuck- up.*

JB. Do you get many in the restaurant?

Qasim. *Aye, quite a few...they go everywhere.*

JB. Do they tip well ?

Qasim. *I dunno...*

JB. Don't you share the tips in the restaurant, then?

Qasim. *No...the manager keeps them.*

JB. I'm surprised by that. I only tip to reward the waiter...I know that visiting American's expect the money to go to the waiter. In the States, the tip is the waiter's wages.

Qasim. *Well...it might be different in different parts of Britain, but here in Scotland the manager keeps them.*

JB. Do you have any brothers and sisters?

104

Qasim. *My brother is in Pakistan. He is studying the Koran. My sister goes to the same school as me. She's in the first year.*

JB. Would you say you were religious?

Qasim. *Aye. Sort of. You know, we're not allowed to drink alcohol and that. I don't think they actually know the system at school. We're not allowed any time for prayers, for instance. In Glasgow it's completely different. You're allowed to go to the Mosque and read whenever you want.*

JB. Do you have any opinion about the Salman Rushdie incident? I've never read his book, I have to say ("the Satanic Verses"). In your family generally was there agreement over the incident ?

Qasim. *Obviously, I heard about it. We talked about it in our family at home...no one is talking about it now! It is just one of those things. I think everyone has got to have the right to criticise every other religion. They are happy to do that here in Scotland...Protestants and Catholics. They hate each other. But there is nothing there! It's just stupid.*

JB. Have you ever been robbed ?

Qasim. *I've got a wee cousin. Fourteen years old. He was at home with his family and a big tall guy came to the door with two other guys. Knocked at the door and said 'have you got any bread?'. A stupid question. And my cousin called to my auntie to lock herself in with the baby and said 'I'll take care of it'. My grandad and my uncle came to the door and there was this guy with a big knife. My grandad closed the door and my uncle got stabbed, but he kicked the knife out of the guys hand and then knocked the guy out!*

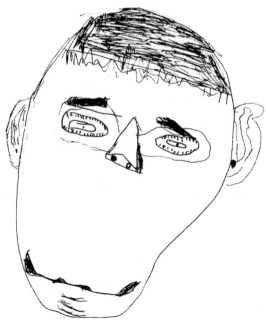

Steven.kirk

James Gibson (Kirkcaldy North)

My dad is special because he takes me camping every year and takes me to play football and we go lots of places. One night my dad came in drunk he come up the stairs and bashed into our toy box. Then he went to his bed and fell out of it. Then he didn't know where the toilet was and had to ask my mum. Then he ordered a bag of chips and when the chips came he went to bed and fell asleep. Me and my mum thought it was funny and kept teasing him and called him drunk. When he's eating a sandwich he just shoves the whole lot of it in. So we call him big mouth and he just smiles. He helps me with my half of the garden. He made a box with a piece of glass over it. I use that in the winter for the sunflowers and my other kinds of flowers. My dad made his own BBQ and we get and lot of burgers and that. Once he was making burgers and that he burnt my one so I swapped my burger for his burger and he ate the burnt one and didn't know and I started laughing. Then one night we had our swimming pool out and he threw me in it. Then he filled the watering can and chased me with it. I was soaking, I went up stairs and my mum was on the phone. I took my shoes off and they were filled with water. My dad come in and started laughing at me. My dad is special to me because he has done a lot of fun things.

Katie Aitken. (Falkland)

My Papa was a very kind man. Every birthday and Christmas he would give us money. He had a lovely house. He lived in Aberdeen. He was my dad's side of the family. He had a wife called Dolly. She died before my dad was born. But something very sad happened. One day my dad had to go up to Aberdeen because Papa was very ill. He was in a home. But he wasn't dying so dad came home. A few days later he died. Everybody was so upset. I still think of him up in heaven.

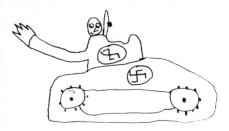

Jonathan Durie (Sinclairtown)

My Grampa was once in the army. He was a General. I try to think what it must have been like in such harsh conditions, with bombs hitting his shelter all the time. I wonder if he ever got shell-shock. I doubt he did…..he is such a great guy.

Paul Woods (Sinclairtown)

This is a story about my dad's dad's dad. He went to see his sister in Africa for a month or two. I never knew until I was born in 1988. It is very magical because I know that when I was born, that was when he went. After that, nobody knew where he went. It was very sad.

Darren Willis (Sinclairtown)

One day my Dad was doing a job and he saw a fire. The firemen's hose got blocked and at that time the fire was a small fire. My step dad offered the firemen a fire extinguisher and the fireman stopped it in about five minutes. The firemen gave my dad some money.. I forgot to tell you. My dad works for the RAC.

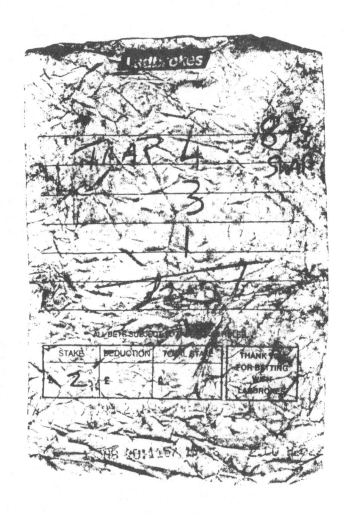

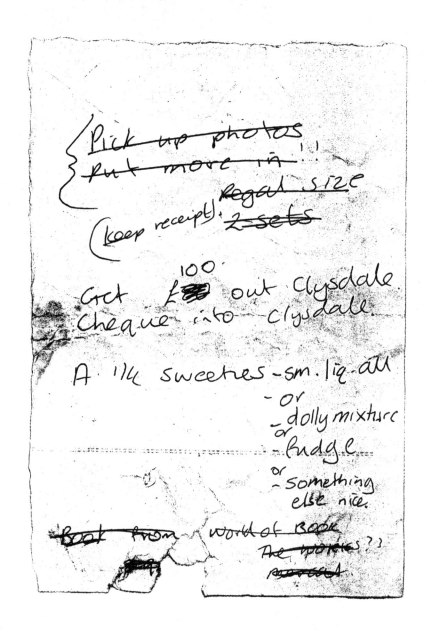

KEN'S
KWIK FRY

KIRKLAND ROAD METHIL
(BEHIND BAYVIEW FOOTBALL PARK)
OPEN EVERY DINNER TIME
12.00am - 2.00pm

OPEN 6 DAYS 5.00pm – 11pm
SUNDAY 5.00pm – 10pm

MENU	Supper	Single
		£1.80
FISH	£2.50	£1.10
SMALL FISH	£1.90	£1.90
SPECIAL FISH	£2.70	£1.60
SCAMPI	£2.30	
CHIPSTEAK	£2.30	
KING RIB	£2.20	
CHICKEN		
CHICKEN BREAST STEAK		
HAMBURGER / IRI...		
OMEL...		

N.B. KEEP THIS BY YOUR PHONE

FAMILY FISH SUPPER £8.50
8 FISH
LOTS OF CHIPS

...ME DELIVERIES WORKS, ETC

		Windygates	£1.00
	Buckhaven £0.70	East Wemyss	£1.00
...0.50	Kennoway £1.20		
	...wn of Wemyss £1.00		

...LEMONADE & CIGARETTES

SCOTTPRINT - METHIL PRINTING

115

Casey Gilliland (Kirkcaldy North)

My gran is very special to me as she saved my life. When I was a baby my mum was feeding me but I started to choke, she tried everything but nothing would work. At that moment my gran came in, took me off my mother, ran been the kitchen, got a teaspoon of ice cold water and made me drink it. It worked I was safe and alive. If it wasn't for my gran I wouldn't be here today. She is always telling me stories about when she was little even then she seemed a nice person. She is always helping people when something is wrong. She has been married for 40 years. My grandad worked in the pit when he was younger. My gran also saved my grandad's life. He had been taken bad nose bleeds for a while, one night it lasted for over two hours but he did not want a doctor in. He went to the toilet, he was in there for over half an hour. My gran was getting worried so she went in. She started to cry, she thought he was dead. She got him down on the floor and started to tap him on the cheeks, he eventually came round. She asked me to talk to him while she phoned the ambulance. I was crying my eves out because I thought he was going to die. The ambulance came a few minutes later and took him to casualty. When he was in the ambulance outside my gran's house they took ages to fix the drip. Me and my gran thought there was something wrong. But he was fine. The next day we went to see him in hospital. He had been taken to a special ward because of an irregular heat-beat. I was so glad when he was all right. If it wasn't for my gran me and my grandad wouldn't be alive. I knew she was put on this planet for some reason. To me, she's the best gran in the world, she's a life saver.

116

Zoe Dodds. (Collydean)

My sister was in a swimming competition. She came 2nd place. She done 25 laps in 10 minutes. She got a medal on the back of the medal it said congratulations you came second. She came down from Dundee and she likes horses. She has one of her own called Snowflake. Snowflake is a lovely horse she has white long hair and clumpy feet.

Grant Porteus. (Falkland)

My Granny Liz had a cat called Cleo. She was a nice cat. When I went down to see my Granny Liz, I let Cleo out down in the field. Sometimes she came back with a deed mouse on the doorstep for a present. Another day she brought back a rat. I was not upset when she died because she sleeped away calmly.

Laura Shanks (Collydean)

My Dad is a D.J. He works for Fife Council and VRN. He went in for a D.J. competition with hospital radio and came first for Scotland and second for Great Britain, in the B.T. Radio awards. His name is Bob Jones and he is really good.

My heroine is Traci Edwards. She is a singer in America and came to visit me in 1996. She is brilliant and could get into the charts soon. She is my Mum's cousin's friend. She has long wavy hair and is a smoker. When I saw her she usually wore jeans and jumpers.

Ross Sneddon (Collydean)

My Grandad got his legs amputated because he was smoking too much. He was smoking fifty a day or more. He got artificial legs from Germany. He still smokes and he has a new house.

Stephen Mitchell (Collydean)

My hero is my Grandad because he was in the war and he got six medals. Some of the stories he tells me are great. He battled at Casino and Dunkirk. One story he told me was when he was in Italy and a scorpion got in his sleeping bag and stung him on the leg and he had to suck the poison out himself. He was also a sergeant-major and one of the medals has got his name on it.

Adam O'Donnell (Collydean)

A few months ago my Auntie Louise separated siamese twins at Yorkhill Hospital. They were joined at the left arm. They both survived and are living happy lives. She did not separate them alone - there were other doctors and nurses involved. My Auntie is my hero because she has also had a pretty rough time of it when a few weeks earlier she was jilted by her fiancee, Hugh.

Michelle Finningham (Collydean)

My special hero is my grandad because he was driving alone in his red mini and came across a burning house which had an old lady and her grandchild inside. My grandad stopped the car and raced across the road to the telephone box and called 999. After five minutes the Firemen arrived and my grandad sat down waiting to see if they got the old lady out. My Grandad said "Is she going to die". Without any answer the Fireman ran back into the house and left him with the lady. My Grandad did first aid for four years, so he began to pump her stomach and her heart began again, but the Grandchild died because smoke went into her lungs. That made my Grandad very sad and sorry for her parents. My Grandad goes and sees the old lady every Monday.

119

Iain Wann. Portrait of Adam O'Donnell. (Collydean)

KIRKCALDY ICE RINK

Presents

ICE REVUE

1948

SOUVENIR
PROGRAMME
1/-

Page Two

KIRKCALDY ICE RINK

Presents

ICE REVUE

1948

SOUVENIR
PROGRAMME
1/-

A list of (Some of) the portrait artists found in this book. (Those that signed their names...)

Katie Aitken
Aktar Ali
Alan (Falkland)
Ruaridh Alan
Colin Beavis
Calum Bell
Denise Bell
Heather Binnie
Bradley (Falkland)
Lenville Burn
Kirsten Burns
Ashliegh Cairns
Calum (Falkland)
Catriona (Falkland)
Melissa Dale
Michele Davies
Laura Dewar
Caroline Dick
Sandy Douglas
Ian Downie
Kirsten Downie
Charlie Duncan
Kirsten Dunnett
Carolyn E.
Amy Edmondson
emma Fairly
Laura Finlay
Michele Finningham
Sharon Fraser
Craig Fyall
Kay Giles
Laura Gordon
Siobhan Greer
Angela Hain
Marian Harley
Alistair Harra
Rachel Harrop
Craig Henderson
Katrina Hynes
Iain (Falkland)
Jenna (Falkland)
Emma Kirby
Stephen Kirk
Lee (Falkland)
Alan L.
James McBain

Lee McCormick
Sheley McDonald
Angela McGuiness
Evonne McKay
Christopher McKellar
Stephanie McLachlan
Kirsten McLaughlin
Kelly McMann
Jocelyn McPhee
Laura Mackle
Jennifer Marshall
Stuart Meacher
Lyndsey Muir
Neil M
Michael Moore
Sarah Motion
Collen Murphy
Gavin Philip
Grant Porteous
Gary Pearson
Jamie Peebles
Rebecca Peebles
Mhairi Rae
Rebecca (Falkland)
Neil Ritchie
Stefan Paul Ruzkai
Kirsty Sala
Pauline Seath
Laura Shanks
David Shaw
Stacy Shaw
Michele Shields
Robyn Smart
Stuart Smith
Debbie Smith
Morgan Smith
Stacy (Falkland)
Thomas Stewart
Jacqueline Syme
Clare Thomson
Gordon Vimpany
Iain Wann
Gemma Watson
James Wilkie
Scot Wilson
Craig Young

Index of contributors.

John Bently and the
Liver and Lights Scriptorium.

In the last decade there has been a huge revival of interest in
The Book as a vehicle for contemporary artists. Initially, the
increased availability of the photocopier and later, all manner
of affordable Information Technology, liberated the means
of production away from huge publishing conglomerates and
galleries and back into the inky hands of spirited individuals.

A new age of passionate pamphleteering was upon us.
Comix, fanzines, tracts, multiples and an unexpected
plethora of mass-produced art in book form. For the artist,
here was a new way of circumnavigating the gallery system:
The book could function as a miniature, portable, exhibition
space, affordable by almost anybody.

As the computer continues to free The Book from it's
traditional role as a mere container of information, it is
becoming an increasingly valid medium of experimentation
and innovation for artists in a way that oddly echoes the
development of painting from a minor to major art form
following the invention of photography in the last century.

John Bently's Liver and Lights series of artists' books has
paralleled these developments since it's inauspicious
beginning as a manifesto-cum-catalogue some twelve years
ago. Meandering through 25 editions so far, each one often
startlingly different in form and concept from its
predecessor, it has developed into a highly personal, richly
hybrid form of art that encompasses, in addition to formal
book making skills, painting, sculpture, history, poetry,
architecture, music, printmaking, performance and much
more besides..

Liver and Lights Scriptorium. Available titles

Liver and Lights no.8. *The one true g'love.* Box, book, beer can and glove. Ed. 110. 1988 £50

The memoirs of a star- blessed derelict of Deptford. The white card box contains fragments of his life in addition to the loose-leaved, hand-coloured book.

Liver and Lights No. 9. *The Billyman.* Box, book, silk flowers, plastic jewels. Ed.210 1990. £30

A sequel to no.8. The Billyman is the embodied spirit of Deptford...

Liver and Lights no 10 *The Ginge.* Box, book, plastic toys, berlin wall fragment. 1990. Ed 100.

Three Editions: Wood inlaid slipcase.   £50
Card box with toys   £30
Wooden hinged altarpiece, painted.   £300

The Ginge is a noted prophet of Deptford. The objects in the box are "the solidified remains of the ginge's famous poem where he mischievously contrasts the Gulf War with the games of children somewhat in the manner of Borges"

Liver and Lights no. 11. *The Beastmaster.* Ed. 50. 1991.£90

Loose-leaf, letterpress and wooden painted boards. A contemporary bestiary set in a post holocaust Deptford.

Liver and Lights No. 14. *A book of discarded things.* Ed. 120 (Two editions) 1992. £30

A book made entirely from rubbish collected from the streets of South London in a gesture of forlorn empathy with all the discarded things of the world.

Liver and Lights no. 15. *The Border Saint.* Ed 70. 1993. £70

Moulded painted reliquary containing book about St Cuthbert..

Liver and Lights No. 20 *Deptfordia.* Ed.70. 1995. £30

Book with hand- painted Tar on cover. Poems about Deptford's infamous history.

Liver and Lights No.22. *The Naming.* Ed.100. 1996. £30

A Box containing continuous drawing with text concerning the origins of language in the context of the prehistoric rock carvings of Northumberland.

Liver and Lights no. 23. *100 Books.* Ed. 100. 1996-99

100 wholly different books each containing a 100 word poem; each poem changed by at least one word. Available May 1999. Send for further details...

Liver and Lights no.s 1-25. The Complete Set.

Includes documentation and subscription forms, posters, exhibition invites etc. Plus various special editions.1984-1999.

£3,000

Also available:

Songs from the Shandy Valley. *Paper back of texts from* **Liver and Lights** *no's 1-10.* Malice Aforethought Press. £5.00

This is a paperback. *A selection of texts from Liver and Lights no.s 12-22, plus manuscript music by Mr Harvey Eagles pertaining to the work's performance. Magpie Press. 1997.* £6.99

All works available from:

Liver and Lights Scriptorium
101 Upland Rd
London
SE22 ODB

Cheques payable to **Liver and Lights**. Postage and packing extra. £2 for one book. £3 for two. £5 for three, over three £7.